Extracts from Aristotle's Works, Selected and Tr. by Georgiana Lady Chatterton
by Aristoteles

Copyright © 2019 by HardPress

Address:
HardPress
8345 NW 66TH ST #2561
MIAMI FL 33166-2626
USA
Email: info@hardpress.net

EXTRACTS
FROM
ARISTOTLE'S WO

02 e. 25

EXTRACTS

FROM

ARISTOTLE'S WORKS.

SELECTED AND TRANSLATED BY
GEORGIANA LADY CHATTERTON.

Printed for Private Circulation by
J. MASTERS AND CO., 78, NEW BOND STREET.
MDCCCLXXV.

12 2 1909

PREFACE.

When I translated passages from Plato's works some years ago, my chief object was to select those which showed his belief in the Soul's immortality and in the happiness resulting from goodness: in fact to show the perception that Plato possessed of some of the high aims and of the eternal happiness that the Christian Revelation afterwards preached and promised.

My object now in selecting the following passages from Aristotle's voluminous works, is to show in another manner the advantage of a belief in Free Will, and to indicate the precepts he advocated for the attainment of happiness even in this world of trial, by means of goodness.

"*Aristotle is the greatest and soundest of Greek Geniuses, and the true founder of science,*" said a learned friend in a kind and encouraging letter just received.

G. C.

February, 1875.

EXTRACTS

FROM

ARISTOTLE'S WORKS.

𝕰𝖙𝖍𝖎𝖈𝖘.

ON THE GOOD AND ON HAPPINESS.

EVERY art, every scientific enquiry, and likewise every action and purpose, appears to aim at some good. Therefore it—the *Good*, has been well defined as that which all things are aiming at.

Different, in some measure, seem to be the ends; for some are energies, and besides or beyond these are some sort of work; but wherever there are certain ends or intentional results beyond the actions, there, and for this reason, these works bring forth results better than the energies.[1] * * *

If therefore there is in all we do some certain End which we desire for its own sake—desiring other things for the sake of that, instead of choosing everything for the sake of something else, (for thus we should go on infinitely, so that our wishes would be vain and trifling,) it is manifest that this must be the Good, and the best and greatest Good.

Is it not therefore of the greatest moment to us, in the conduct of our lives,

[1] This seems to express that it is better to have a constant good intention, and thus by a permanent effort or Will, be more able to attain the object, than by energy or spontaneous effort, which however powerful at the time, may not be constant or energising enough to attain the end proposed.

that we should have a knowledge of this? And if, like archers, we aim at a mark, shall we not be more likely to attain what we wish to obtain? Now if it be so, we should try to enclose in an outline and give a sketch, and determine to what science or art it [this End] belongs. * * *

Now each person judges rightly of what he knows; and of those things he is a good judge. He then who is well instructed in each science judges well of that science, and universally he who has been instructed in them all. But on this account a young man is not a fit student of politics, for he is inexperienced in the actions of life, (which are the subjects of this treatise.) Moreover, being inclined to follow the dictates of passion, he will hear in vain and without profit, since the end of the political art is not knowledge but practice. There is no difference whether he is a youth in age, or a youth in character. For the incapacity is not of time, [or rather want of age,] but from his manner of life and pursuits being influenced by passion; for to such persons knowledge becomes useless, as it does to the licentious or to those who have no power over their own passions. But those who, according to reason, earnestly desire to know these subjects, may do much good in many ways by hearing and following these precepts.

Concerning the student, or how he is to accept our argument, and what we propose to show, let this much be prefaced. * * *

Since all knowledge and deliberate preference aims at some good, let us show what [that] which we call the political science aims at, and what is the highest practice or result of goodness. Its name, indeed, is not difficult to define, for most people, both the gifted and the masses call it Happiness. But they suppose that to live well and to act well are the same as to be happy.

Concerning the nature of happiness, or in what happiness consists, they are at variance; the masses or vulgar do not give the same definition of it as the wise and educated, for some suppose it to be an obvious and clearly defined object—such as pleasures, riches, or honours. Others attribute it to other things, and often the same person thinks differently about it at different times, for when ill, he imagines it to be health, when poor, wealth; but conscious of their own ignorance, they admire those who say it is something great and far above them. Some indeed have supposed that besides all these good things there is another self-existent Good, which is the cause of their being good. * * *

But let us not forget that arguments from principles or to principles are different. For well did Plato also evince doubts on this point, and enquired or sought whether the right way is from principles [or beginnings] or to principles, just as in the racecourse whether from the starting point to the goal or the contrary. For we must begin from the things that are known, and they are known in two ways; for some are known to ourselves and absolutely, and others are generally known. Perhaps, then, we should begin from the things known to ourselves.

Therefore whoever is to study well the

things which are good and just, in fact, the subjects of political science, must have been well and morally educated, for the point from whence we must begin is the Fact, and if this is satisfactorily proved it will not be necessary to add the reason. Such a student possesses or would easily acquire the principles. But let him who does not profess either of these qualifications,[1] hear what Hesiod says,

"He above all men is the best, and to himself a friend, who from his own wisdom deems the present time the best

To attain the end. And good is he, who revolving in his mind, obeys the words of wisdom.

But whoso is not wise himself nor will consider well

[1] That is, humility, and a desire to know what is good and virtuous.

The wise counsel given by others, he indeed is a most useless man." * * *

Let us return to the point; for men seem not unreasonably to judge of *the Good* and of Happiness from observing the different lives of men. The numerous common and uneducated people suppose it to be pleasure, and these are satisfied with a life of enjoyment.

For there are three kinds of lives which are most evident; first, that now mentioned, then the political, and thirdly, the contemplative.

Now the common or vulgar people who are entirely slavish, deliberately choose the life of brutes, but they find a reason for this, because many persons in authority are led by the same passions, as Sardanapalus.

But well educated persons, liking active

pursuits, suppose it to be honour, and deem this to be the end or object of political life; but it appears to be too superficial for the object of our search: for it, that is, Happiness seems to be more with those who confer, than with those who receive honour. But we naturally conceive that "the Good" is something peculiarly one's own, and difficult to be taken away from us. Men seem to pursue honour that they may believe themselves to be good. They seek to be honoured by wise men, and by their acquaintances, on account of virtue; it is therefore evident, that in their opinion, virtue itself is superior [to honour].   *   *   *

But a life of striving for riches is against our natural inclinations, and riches are evidently not "the Good" we are in search of, for they are merely useful for the sake of some other end or object. * * *

Again, since *the Good* is found in as many ways as Existence or Being, for it is predicated in Essence as in God and Intellect; and in Quality, as the Virtues; and in Quantity, as the Mean or Moderate; and in Relation, as Utility; and in Time, as Opportunity; and in Place, as Habitation, &c., &c., it is evident it cannot be anything common, universal, alone. For then it would not have been predicated in all these categories, but in one only. * * *

Now the Good we are searching for, seems to be different in different courses of action and arts. * * *

But in every action of deliberate preference, it must be the End, since for the sake of this we do everything. * * *

But the chief Good appears to be something perfect, so that if there is any end which is alone perfect that must be the very thing we are in search of, but if there are many it must be the most perfect of them. Now we think that the object pursued for its own sake is more perfect than that pursued for another; and that the object not chosen on account of another thing is more perfect than those which are eligible both by themselves and for the sake of that other. In fact we deem that entirely and completely perfect which is always chosen for its own sake, and not on account of anything else.

It appears indeed that self-sufficingness —[or rather mastery over oneself] for the perfect Good, seems to be sufficient to itself, but we attribute self-sufficingness not to him who leads for himself alone a solitary life, but to him who lives also for his parents or children, and wife, and also for his friends and fellow-citizens; since man is naturally a social being. * * *

The " self-sufficing" we define as that which suffices to itself, and separated from everything else, makes life eligible and wanting nothing; and this we suppose the nature of happiness to be; and moreover we suppose it the most eligible of all things; when not reckoned with any other good. * * *

Happiness then seems to be something perfect and self-sufficient, being the end and object of all human actions. * * *

Now if the work of man is an energy [a zealous eagerness] of the soul, according to reason, and not without reason, and if we say that man's work, done well and zealously is of the same kind, as in the case of a harper and a good harper, (and so, in all cases, superiority in each particular excellence being added to each particular work;) for it is the work of a harper to play, and of a good harper to play well; and if we assume the work of man to be a kind of life, and this life an energy of the soul, and actions performed with reason; and the peculiar work of a good man to be the same thing done well and honourably; everything to be complete according to its proper excellence; if, I say, this is true, it follows that man's chief good is *An energy of the soul according to virtue;* but if the virtues are many, then it must be according to the best and most perfect virtue. And besides this, [it must last for] a perfect and entire life; for as a spring or summer is not made by one swallow, or one day, neither one day nor a short time makes a man blessed or happy. * * *

Now "Good" being divided into three classes,[1] some being external, others said to belong to the soul, and others to the body, we deem those belonging to the soul the superior, and good, in a higher sense than the others; but we assume that the actions and energies of the soul belong to the soul. So that according to this opinion, which is ancient and allowed by the philosophers, our assertion would be right that certain actions and energies are the end [or object]; for thus it becomes one of the goods of the soul, and not one of the external ones. Also that the happy man lives well, [or rather does good,] and

[1] According to the ancient philosophers that preceded Aristotle.

acts well, agrees with our definition, for we almost defined happiness as a kind of well-living and well-acting.

It appears again, that all the qualities required for happiness exist in our definition. To some it seems to be virtue, to others prudence, to others a kind of wisdom; to some indeed these or some of them added to pleasure, or not without pleasure. But others include external prosperity; but of these notions many ancient writers support some, a few celebrated philosophers support the others; but we may suppose that none of them are quite wrong, and in some one particular they are for the most part right. * * *

But as in the Olympic Games, it is not the most beautiful and strongest who are crowned, but those who strive to win, (yet some of these conquer,) in such a manner it is only those who act right, and lead good lives, who can attain that which is honourable. And their life itself is pleasant, for to be happy is one of the goods of the soul, because it is pleasant to any one to possess what he loves best.[1]

The lover of justice loves best what is just, and the lover of virtue virtuous things. * * *

So that these men are pleased even of themselves; their life therefore does not need the addition of pleasure as a kind of amulet [appendage], but possesses pleasure in itself. Besides, as we have said, that man is not good who does not rejoice in honourable and good actions. * * *

---

[1] I.e., loving virtue, his greatest pleasure must be the pursuit and attainment of it, as Aristotle says in the next sentence.

For we could not call that man good who takes no pleasure in good actions, nor a liberal man, one who does not rejoice in liberal actions, and in other cases the same. And if this be so, the actions of virtue must be pleasant in themselves.

Therefore the best, most beautiful, and meetest thing is this kind of happiness. * * *

Now if indeed there is any other thing which God gives to man, it is reasonable to suppose that happiness is a Divine gift; for it, of all human things, is the best. * * *

For the prize and end of virtue appears to be something that is best, Godlike and blessed. It must be enjoyed by many; for by teaching and care it may exist in every person who is not without power to become virtuous. * * *

For happiness is a kind of energy, or ever striving hard of the soul, for the attainment of virtue. * * *

Most essential are virtuous energies for happiness, and the contrary produce the contrary—witness the question we have discussed; for stability does not exist in any human thing so much as in virtuous energies; more permanent indeed these seem to be than even the sciences, and the most honourable of them are likewise the more stable, because happy men most especially and constantly pass their lives in them; and this seems to be the reason why they never forget them. Therefore the thing we are in search of, [i.e., permanent happiness,] will exist in the virtuously happy man, and therefore through life he will remain so; for he always, and most of all men will live in the contemplation of virtuous actions, and he will bear the accidents of fortune most nobly, and in every case suitably, as a man perfectly good. * * *

When he meets with great misfortunes, the honourable character is conspicuous, for he will bear them with equanimity, not from insensibility, but because he is brave and high-souled. And if the virtuous energies rule his life, he can never become miserable, for he can never do hurtful and worthless actions. * * *

If this is the case, the man who is happy in this way can never become miserable. * * *

What then prevents us from pronouncing that man happy who energizes [or exerts incessantly all his faculties] according to perfect virtue?

By human happiness we mean not that

of the body, but of the Soul, and this, as we said before, is an energy of the soul according to perfect virtue. * * *

There seems to be in man something else by nature contrary to reason, which contends with and resists reason. We praise the wise man according to his habits; and praiseworthy habits we call virtues. * * *

It does not therefore make a slight, but an important difference, whether we have been brought up in these, or in other habits from childhood. * * *

Virtue therefore is a habit, accompanied with deliberate preference, defined by reason and as the prudent man would define it. * * *

But much depends on moderation, or the just mean, and therefore it is difficult to be good; just as it is not in every man's power, but only in the power of him who knows how, to find the centre of a circle. * * *

It is therefore necessary for him who aims at the just mean, first to keep away from that extreme that is more contrary. * * But in every case we must be most upon our guard against what is pleasant, and pleasure; for we are not unbiassed judges of it. * * *

It is necessary for those who study the subject of virtue, to define what actions are voluntary, and what are involuntary, and it is necessary that Legislators should do so, for the regulation of rewards and punishments. * * *

ON FREE WILL.

THERE seems to be a difference between acting through ignorance, and acting foolishly [or without mind.]

For a drunken or angry man does not think he is acting ignorantly; yet a vicious man is really ignorant or without mind about what he ought to do, and from what he ought to abstain. Through such faulty ignorance men become unjust and entirely depraved. * * *

We get our character from our deliberate preference of things good and bad. * * *

The good man's object of volition is really good, but the bad man's is anything that he may happen at the moment to think good, * * for the good man judges everything rightly, and in every case the real truth appears so to him. * * *

But the generality of mankind seem to be deceived by pleasure; for it appears to them to be the good, though it is not so. These men choose what is pleasant, mistaking present pleasure for the good which produces happiness, and fly from pain [or self-denial] as from an evil. * * *

Vice is voluntary, or else we must contradict what we have just said, and deny that man has free will, and is the parent and origin of his own actions as he is of his children. * * *

The punishment is double for drunken people; for the principle is in themselves, since it was in their own power not to get drunk; and this is the cause of their ignorance. * * *

And in all other cases they appear to be ignorant through negligence, when it was in their own power not to be ignorant; for they could have paid attention to good precepts. And when persons are unable to give their attention, or hearken to good advice, they are themselves the causes of their inability to attend, by living in a dissipated manner, and are also the cause themselves of their being unjust, of performing bad actions, and being intemperate, by passing their time in drinking bouts and such like. * * *

Virtue is voluntary, and vice is just as voluntary as virtue, for the bad man is just as voluntary an agent in his actions as a good man.

ON FRIENDSHIP.

FRIENDSHIP is a kind of virtue, or joined with virtue, and is quite necessary for life. Without friends no one would choose to live even if he possessed all other goods. For to the rich, and to those in office and authority Friends seem to be most needful; for what is the use of such good fortune if the power to bestow benefits is taken away, which is exerted in the most praiseworthy manner, and principally towards friends? And how could it be preserved and kept safe without friends? For the more it abounds, the more insecure it becomes. And in poverty and other misfortunes our only refuge seems to be our friends. To the young friendship is most necessary in order to keep them from error; and to the old, as a consolation, and to assist that which is deficient in their actions on account of weakness; and to those who are at the height of their powers, to further their good deeds, as the poet [Homer] says,

"When two meet each other"
they are more able to conceive and to execute. * * *

The friendship of the good then is friendship in the highest degree, for that which is absolutely good and meet is an object of love and choice. * * *

Good temper and sociability seem to belong to friendship and to produce it in the greatest degree. * * *

But friendship seems really to consist more in loving than in being loved. A sign of this is that Mothers rejoice in loving. For some give their children to be nursed, and knowing that they are their own, love them, though they may not seek to be loved in return, if both cannot be. But it seems sufficient to them their thriving well, and they continue to love even if their children, through ignorance, cannot repay what is due to their Mother. * * *

In this manner those who are unlike each other or unequal, may be the greatest friends; for they may be equalized. But those who are similar are more likely to become friends, and particularly those who possess the similarity of virtue; for as they have stability in themselves they possess also the same towards each other, and they neither ask nor render base services. But we may say indeed, that they even prevent such; for the really good neither commit faults themselves nor allow their friends to commit them. The wicked have no stability, for they do not continue consistent even with themselves. * * *

ON RELATIVE DUTIES.

It would seem that we ought to assist our parents, more than any one else, by serving or supporting them, being in fact their debtors, and because it is more honourable to assist those who gave us birth than ourselves. We should also give honour to our parents as to the Gods. * * *

We should also give to every old man the honour due to his age, by standing up in his presence, and giving him the most honourable place, and such like marks of respect. * * *

The friendship of the good is most advantageous, for they appear to become better by energising, that is, exerting all their best faculties, and correcting one another, for they receive an impress from each other in whatever is most advantageous, as it is said:

"What is good will be learnt from the giver." * * *

ON PLEASURE.

AFTER Friendship, we may proceed with the subject of Pleasure; for it seems to be most intimately connected with our nature. By this we educate the young, stirring them by pleasure and pain. It seems to be most important in laying the foundation of the moral character, that men should rejoice in those things wherein they ought to rejoice, and hate what they ought to hate: having influence during their whole lives on the side of virtue and a happy life. * * *

To be zealous and to labour for the sake of amusement appears foolish and childlike. But to amuse ourselves in order to work zealously and well, as Anacharsis said, seems to be right. For amusement is like relaxation, and therefore it is not the end : for we have recourse to it to re-create the energies. But the happy life is according to virtue, and this is zealous and energetic, but does not consist in amusement or play. * * *

If happiness is an energy according to virtue, we may well say it must be the best, and this must be the virtue of the best part of man. * * This energy is contemplative * * and the wise man even when alone, is able to enjoy contemplation. * * *

But a man ought not to entertain human thoughts, as some would advise, because he is human, nor mortal thoughts because he is mortal, but he should try to make himself immortal, and do everything with the object of living in accordance with the best and highest principle in him. * * *

We must not imagine that a person who is to be happy will require many and great Goods. * * It is possible to perform honourable and good actions without being Lord of the Earth and Sea; for any one with moderate means may be able to act according to virtue. * * *

Now if we have said enough about virtue and friendship and pleasure [or rather happiness] can we deem that our original intention is completed? Or is the end and object of our actions not the contemplation and knowledge of all things, but rather the practice and fulfilment of them? If so, it is not enough to know the theory of virtue, but we must try to possess and employ it; and pursue whatever other means there may be to become good.

Now if treatises were sufficient of themselves to make men good, they would indeed have received many great rewards, as Theognis says :

"If to the sons of Æsculapius it had been given
To cure the vices and bad hearts of men
Many and great would their rewards have been."

And we ought to provide ourselves with them. But it appears indeed, that they have the power to urge on and excite young men who have naturally a love of truth and goodness, to be easily influenced by virtue: but that they have no power to persuade the multitude [or masses] to pursue what is good and honourable. For the masses are incapable of being influenced by shame, but only by fear, nor of abstaining from vicious actions because they are disgraceful, but from fear of punishment; for while they live, they are under the influence of their passions, and pursue their own peculiar pleasures, and the means of gratifying them. They also avoid what is painful; but of what is honourable and tends to happiness they have no idea, because they never had a taste for it. What reasoning then can change such men as these? for it is scarcely possible or at least not easy to alter by persuasion what has been impressed for a long time on the moral character. * * *

Metaphysics.

ALL men are naturally desirous of Knowledge. A sign [or proof] of this is our love [or value] of the senses, and even without regard to their utility they are loved for their own sakes, and most of all the rest, the sense of sight. Not alone for practical purposes, but also when we are not intent on doing anything, we choose the sense of vision in preference —so to say—above all the rest of our senses. The reason of this is, that this one of our senses enables us most to comprehend the distinct or different qualities manifested by it. * * *

Now by memory experience is produced among men, for by repeated acts of memory about the same thing done, the power of a single experience is perfected. And it seems that science and art are almost similar to experience. For science and art are produced by experience among men. For experience indeed, as Polus says (and rightly so) has produced art, but inexperience—chance. An art then comes into being when out of many experiences, one universal opinion is evolved out of similar cases. * * *

At present the reason of our making this treatise is the fact that all consider what is called Wisdom is to be conversant about first causes and principles; so that —as before said—the experienced seem to be more wise than those who possess any other sense. * * *

That indeed Wisdom is therefore a Science, conversant about certain causes and first principles, is obvious. * * *

Now since we are seeking to investigate the science, this must be the subject of our consideration, namely, with what kind of causes this science, I mean wisdom, is conversant. * * *

Now we suppose in the first place, that the wise man especially is acquainted with all things scientifically, if this is possible, not however having a scientific knowledge of them singly. In the next place a person who is able to know things that are difficult, and not easy for a man to understand, such a one we deem wise. * * *

It is evident that we seek scientific knowledge from no other ground of utility save what springs from itself. But as we say a free man exists, who is such, for his own sake and not for another, so also, this alone of the sciences is free, for this alone subsists, or is sought for its own sake. Wherefore also we may judge that the acquisition of this science is not human, for in many cases human nature is servile, [a slave to human passions and incapacities.] So that according to Simonides the Deity alone should enjoy this gift: yet it is unworthy for a man not to investigate the knowledge that concerns his own condition. * * *

Nor ought we to deem any other science more to be praised as under our present consideration. For that which is most divine is also the most to be honoured, and can be attained only in two ways; for that which most belongs to the Deity is a divine one among the sciences. * * *

For to all speculators does the Deity appear as a Cause, and a certain First Principle: and either God alone, or He principally, would possess such a science as this. Therefore it is possible that all other sciences may be more practically useful than this one, but none is more excellent. * * *

Since then it is evident that we ought to be in possession of a science of primary causes * * therefore, though there has been enough speculation about this in our treatise on Physics, let us however bring forward those who before our time have approached to our examination of the entities, and have philosophized [formed systems of philosophy] respecting Truth. For it is manifest that they also maintain that certain first principles and causes exist. Therefore it will be of use to our present purpose, if we review these philosophers, for we shall thereby discover either a certain different description of cause, or repose our confidence by preference in those that we have already enumerated. Now most of those who first formed systems of philosophy consider those that subsist in the form of matter to be alone or solely the principles of all things, wherefrom all entities arise, and wherefrom they are generated, as from an original, and whereto they are corrupted—the substance ultimately indeed remaining permanent, but undergoing a change in its passive states. This [matter] they assert to be an element, and this a first principle of all things. And for this reason they think that nothing is

Metaphysics. 43

either produced or destroyed, because such a constitution of nature is always in a state of conservation.[1] * * *

[Aristotle, after describing the speculations of a number of early philosophers, says:]

But after these philosophers, and after the assertion of these kind of principles—as if by reason of their insufficiency to generate the nature of entities, [Beings, or existing things,] again obliged by actual truth, as we have said, they investigated the principle next following as a consequence. For the good and beautiful order of some things, and the production of others of the entities, it is not easy to

---

[1] What an old theory, of the infancy of Philosophy, our modern materialists in their unoriginal stupidity seem to have adopted! See also the modern automaton theory mentioned and condemned by Aristotle.

suppose that either fire, or earth, or anything of this kind is their Cause, nor is it likely these men should think it is. Nor was it seemly on the other hand, to deem that they were self-made, i.e., automata, nor to attribute such important and beautiful things and beings to chance.

Whoever affirmed that mind is the cause of the whole system of the world and of living beings, and of the entire harmony of it all, the same appeared indeed to judge discreetly in comparison with the vain theorists of the earlier ages.[1]

It is evident indeed that Anaxagoras

---

[1] I.e., the materialists, who attributed, as our modern scientific men do, all things to chance, and even suppose that human beings are automata—machines wound up and consequently devoid of free will.

adopted this view, [that mind was the cause and origin of all things.] Hermotimus of Clazomenæ, however, has the credit of having adopted this theory at an earlier period. Those indeed who have held these opinions concerning mind, have laid it down as a first principle of entities, and the cause of their beautiful and orderly arrangement also as the origin of motion in things. * * *

Some one might suppose that Hesiod was the first to seek this cause, [i.e. mind,] and that this is the case with whatever other speculation that may have deemed Love as a first principle in entities, as Parmenides did; for this philosopher, in describing his scheme of the generation of the universe, says:

"The first Divine principle was Love."

But Hesiod's words were:

"First in order Chaos came, and then
The spacious Earth,
Then Love, distinguished amongst all the immortals." * * *

Parmenides, however, seems to adopt a system of unity according to reason [or mind,] whereas Melissus adopted a theory according to matter. * * *

Xenophanes first introduced this system of unity, (for Parmenides is said to have been his pupil,) but made nothing plain, neither did he seem to have understood either of these systems, but looking wistfully on the whole Heaven, he affirms that Unity is God. * * *

After these said philosophers Plato's system comes, in many points following the views of the Pythagoreans, but having also peculiar tenets of his own, differing from the philosophy of the Italics. * * *

The cause of the "Good and the Bad," or the "Well and the Evil," he attributed severally to several elements, or first principles, which we affirm that certain philosophers, such as Empedocles and Anaxagoras, have investigated more elaborately than any of the early speculators. * * *

They indeed who assign mind, or Love, as a final cause of actions, and changes, and motions, deem it to be something that is *Good*. * * *

Further, it is necessary that substances, or elements, should not involve a connection with matter. For it is requisite that they should be eternal, if indeed there is anything everlasting. It is then in energy [a working vivid spirit] that they subsist. * * *

Of necessity the Immoveable First Mover must constitute an Entity or Being, and inasmuch as it necessarily subsists, it therefore must subsist after an excellent beautiful manner, and in this way becomes a first principle of force. * * *

From a first principle therefore of this kind, one that involved the principle of a first mover, has arisen Heaven and Nature. * * *

The first Mover must continue in the enjoyment of the principle of life for ever. * * In this way is the Deity disposed as to existence, and the principle of life is inherent in the Deity, for the energy or active existence of Mind constitutes life, and God, as we have shown, constitutes this energy, and essential energy belongs to God, as His best and everlasting life. Therefore we affirm that the Deity is a Being that is everlasting and most excellent in nature: so that His life and duration are uninterrupted and eternal. Such is the very essence of God. * * *

Anaxagoras regarded what is *"good"* as a first principle, so far as it is a power that imparts motion. * * *

Physics.

[THE origin of all things and first causes are more fully discussed in Aristotle's Physics, which has, I am told, never been translated into English. I will now quote the following short passages, and hope some day to translate the whole work.]

Since then movement must always be, and cannot be interrupted, it is necessary that there be something which first moves [other things], whether it be one or many —to wit, That first Immoveable Mover.

Therefore it makes nothing against this reasoning, that every one of those things which are themselves immoveable, yet move other things, are eternal; but the necessity that there should be something which is indeed itself immoveable and free from external change, as well simply as accidentally, will thus appear manifest to those who consider. * * *

We must now explain why this [i.e., the first and immoveable Mover] is without parts, and has no magnitude. But, first of all, we will define those things that come first; and one of them is this:

That which is finite cannot move [something else] in infinite time.

There are three things [to be considered here]: The mover, the moved, and that *in* which it is moved, viz., Time. Now either these are all three infinite, or all three finite, or else two or one are. * * *

From what has been defined it appears

clearly to be impossible that the first and immoveable Mover should have any magnitude; for if it has magnitude, it must necessarily be either finite or infinite. Now it has been proved before, in the Physics, that there cannot be an infinite magnitude, and it has now been proved that a finite magnitude cannot have an infinite force, nor the finite move anything in infinite time. But the first Mover effects eternal motion, and in infinite time. Clearly, therefore, it is indivisible and without parts, and has no magnitude. * * *

Politics.

THERE is in all persons a natural wish to associate with each other, and whoever first established civil society was the cause of the greatest good. For as man thus civilized and perfected is the best and most excellent of all living beings, so without law and justice he is the worst and most savage of them all. For nothing is so savage as armed injustice, but man can by nature acquire the arms of prudence and virtue. Or on the contrary, he may acquire arms for the most opposite purposes. And therefore he will be the most wicked and cruel who is devoid of virtue—also the most unholy and savage being imaginable. Now justice is a social virtue, for it is the rule of the social state and the most righteous of judgments. * * *

No one could pronounce that man blessed or happy who is devoid of fortitude or temperance, justice or prudence. * * It is easy to prove from the teaching of experience that virtue is not acquired by means of external goods; although it is possible that they may be acquired by means of virtue. As to a happy life, whether it be founded in pleasure, or in prudence, or in both, it certainly belongs more often to those whose morals are most pure, and whose understandings are best cultivated—who are moderate in the acquisition of worldly Goods—than it does to those who possess a sufficiency of worldly Goods, but who are deficient in these virtuous qualities. * * *

Let us therefore remember that happiness falls to the lot of each person according to the wisdom and virtue he possesses, and in proportion as he acts according to their dictates. We have the example of God Himself for this, who is completely happy, not from any external good, but in Himself, and by nature. For good fortune, and worldly possessions, are things necessarily different from happiness, as every external good is produced by chance or luck. But it is not by chance that any one is just or wise. * * No one can fare well who does not act well; nor can the actions of a man, or of a city, or country, be praised as worthy, without virtue or wisdom. But courage, justice, and wisdom, have in a state the same power and force as in persons, and it is only in proportion as he possesses these virtues that each man is deemed just, wise, and prudent. * * *

To prefer idleness to activity is also wrong, for happiness consists in action, and many noble ends are produced by the actions of just and wise men. * * *

[After advising as to the choice of the best situations for towns and houses, Aristotle says:]

Care should be taken that there should be a plentiful supply of water, and rivers near at hand, but if these cannot be found, very large and immense cisterns should be prepared to receive all the rain water. * * And as great care should be taken of the health of the inhabitants, the first requisite is, that the city should have a good situation and position; the second is, that there may be good water to drink; and this which we are to drink must not be cared for as a secondary matter. For what we chiefly and most frequently use for the support of the body, must principally contribute to its health; and this is the influence which the air and water naturally have. For this reason in all wise governments the water ought to be appropriated to different purposes, if all the supplies are not equally good; and if there is not a plentiful supply of each kind of water, that which is to drink should be separated from that which is for other uses. * * *

Rhetoric.

ALMOST every one individually and all men in general have some object at which they direct every aim, and which they choose or avoid. And this, to speak summarily, is Happiness and its constituents. Therefore, for the sake of example, let us find out what happiness in general is, and in what it consists. For with the subject of it, and with what conduces to it, and its opposites, the exhortation of an orator is [or must be] always conversant. * * Among some of the constituents of happiness, Learning and Admiring are pleasant to most people, for what is admired is desired or loved: and the act of learning, or to learn, and to become acquainted with everything is a natural desire. And to do good, that is, to benefit others, or to be benefited by them, is pleasant.

And because a tendency to beneficence is pleasant, it is also gratifying to set a neighbour on his legs again, and to complete what was deficient in some particular. And as the acquaintance of knowledge is pleasant, and to contemplate [things or persons] with admiration is pleasant, that too must necessarily be pleasant which has been expressed in imitation, as in Painting, Sculpture, and Poetry. Also it is pleasant to contemplate anything that has been correctly imitated, although the original object of which it is the imitation may not in itself be pleasant or to be admired. * * *

About friendship and hatred. Let us define the reasons which produce friendship and the act of cherishing this feeling.

To have a friendly feeling may be defined as wishing something we think good to a person for his sake and not for our own, and, as far as we can, exerting ourselves to procure it. And a friend is he who entertains and meets a return of this feeling.

This being the case, of necessity it must be that one who participates in another's joy and good fortune, and in sorrow at what pains him, not from any other motive, but only as his friend, exercises true friendship. * * Those too, are friends, to whom some things become good and the same evil. So that he who wishes for another what he does for himself, appears to be a friend to that other. * * *

CONCERNING FEAR.

Now fear should be defined as a kind of pain or agitation of the fancy, an idea that an evil, capable of either destroying or giving pain, is impending over us. People do not fear every evil; for instance, a man does not fear lest he should become unjust or stupid, but people fear all the evils whose effect is either much pain, or destruction, or these only when they do not seem to be far removed, but give the idea of being about to happen. They do not fear that which they think seems very far off, for all know that they shall die; but as the event does not seem to be near, they do not think about it.

SHAME AND SENSITIVENESS, IN-SENSIBILITY AND IMPUDENCE.

A SENSE of Shame should be defined as a kind of pain and agitation about evils present, past, and to come which seem to tend to a loss of character: and impudence to be a kind of neglect and apathy about these points. Now, if the sensibility to the pain or agitation we have mentioned, is that which causes shame, it must follow that a man must feel it on the occurrence of evils of a kind which appear to be disgraceful, either to himself or those whom he esteems. * * *

All cowardice is a source of Shame. * * It is also shameful not to work or endure toils which those who are advanced in years, or who have been delicately nurtured, or who are of higher rank, or whose strength is inferior to one's own can endure, because all this shows effeminacy. And so it is to be benefited by another and that often; or to reproach a person with his obligations to you. For this shows a mean and abject spirit. Also to talk about oneself and to triumph about praises of oneself, and to pretend that to be one's own which belongs to another [or to appear richer than we are.] These are indications of arrogance.

Poetics.

TRAGEDY is an imitation of a serious or perfect action having magnitude, composed in pleasant language, with the different kinds of imitation separate in their parts, and acted, not narrated, and effecting through pity and fear a purification from such passions as it portrays.[1] By pleasing language I mean language, passion, rhythm, harmony, and melody, and using separately the several species of

---

[1] By thus acting and exciting among the audience pity and fear, this counteracts and purifies the effect of the bad passions in some of the characters represented in the working out of the Story, and calls forth the high and good qualities of the others.

imitation, because some parts of the Tragedy are perfected by metre, and the others through melody.

Check Out More Titles From HardPress Classics Series In this collection we are offering thousands of classic and hard to find books. This series spans a vast array of subjects – so you are bound to find something of interest to enjoy reading and learning about.

Subjects:
Architecture
Art
Biography & Autobiography
Body, Mind &Spirit
Children & Young Adult
Dramas
Education
Fiction
History
Language Arts & Disciplines
Law
Literary Collections
Music
Poetry
Psychology
Science
…and many more.

Visit us at www.hardpress.net

Im The Story
personalised classic books

"Beautiful gift.. lovely finish. My Niece loves it, so precious!"

Helen R Brumfieldon

★★★★★

UNIQUE GIFT
FOR KIDS, PARTNERS AND FRIENDS

Timeless books such as:

Kids

Alice in Wonderland • The Jungle Book • The Wonderful Wizard of Oz
Peter and Wendy • Robin Hood • The Prince and The Pauper
The Railway Children • Treasure Island • A Christmas Carol

Adults

Romeo and Juliet • Dracula

- **Highly** Customizable
- **Change** Books Title
- **Replace** Characters Names with yours
- **Upload** Photo for inside page
- **Add** Inscriptions

Visit **ImTheStory**.com
and order yours today!